Rug Hooker's Companion

by Donna Hrkman

Published by
STACKPOLE BOOKS
5067 Ritter Road
Mechanicsburg, PA 17055
www.stackpolebooks.com

Printed in the United States

10 9 8 7 6 5 4 3 2 1

First edition

Cover design by Caroline Stover
Cover rug by Donna Hrkman
Cover photo by Impact Xpozures
All illustrations by Donna Hrkman

Library of Congress Cataloging-in-Publication Data

Hrkman, Donna.
 Rug hooker's companion / by Donna Hrkman, Rug hooking magazine. —
1st ed.
    p. cm.
 Includes bibliographical references.
 ISBN 978-1-881982-83-8
 1. Rugs, Hooked. I. Rug Hooking Magazine. II. Title.
 TT850.H75 2003
 746.7'4—dc23
                        2012005526

Contents

Introduction

Welcome to Rug Hooker's Companion

WHAT IS RUG HOOKING?

I'm hooked on wool, she admitted sheepishly...

Rug hooking is the art of creating designs by pulling colored strips of wool or other fabric through an evenweave fabric foundation, like burlap or linen, using a small-tipped metal hook with a handle. The loops that are formed make up the surface of the rug.

This little handbook is loaded with information about the fine art of making hooked wool rugs. A handy guide for beginners as well as experienced rug hookers, the *Companion* was created to provide easy-to-find facts and information all in one compact source.

Use it as you would use a dictionary for quick definitions of a term or hooking-related word you aren't familiar with, or use it to compile a shopping list when you're starting a new project. You'll find illustrations to help you make sense of some of the processes, as well as concise definitions for terms and materials.

The *Companion* includes something for everyone, with sections about basic tools, dye materials, different kinds of wool, and maybe even some rug-related facts you've never thought about. It's a fun and informative look at the art we love to create.

Welcome to the art of rug hooking, or as we call it, "painting with wool."

Chapter 1

The Rug

Some common components identify specific rug parts. The most basic of these terms are used when describing sections of the rug.

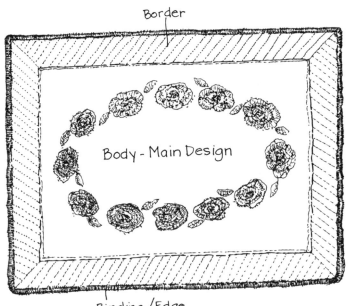

Parts of a rug

Body

The body is the main portion of the rug or the area that is the primary focus. This space contains most of the design elements, but these elements can be carried over into a border as well. Some rugs are hooked without any border, making the body of the rug the whole image.

Border

The border is the area surrounding the main body of the rug. A border design can visually contain the inner design and complement it. The width of the border is decided at the whim of the rug maker and can vary from no border at all to borders of any width. Rug hookers may also choose not to add a border at all.

Borders are commonly found on Oriental style rugs, which incorporate geometric motifs, and are also used to repeat design elements in other rug styles. Borders can be irregularly hooked to create a stylized edge instead of being hooked in straight lines.

Some border designs are hooked to look like actual picture frames.

When calculating a border width for your rug, see "How Much Foundation Do I Need" in chapter 6 (page 37).

Binding

The edges of rugs need to be finished in a way that protects the exposed edge from wear and supports the outside row of loops. Rug hookers have developed several ways to bind their rugs.

One method is to sew flat, ribbon-like rug binding to the outside edge of the pattern before beginning to hook. When the hooking is finished, the binding is folded to the back, tacked down, and sewn flat to protect the edge.

Another method is to turn the edges over a cotton cord and whip them with yarn.

Other decorative binding techniques provide a more elaborate or fancier look, including crochet, braiding, or wrapping the cotton cord with strips of wool instead of yarn. You'll find more details about binding in chapter 13.

> *"Hooking isn't entirely a feminine pursuit, either. It is one form of needlecraft that a man can work at without being regarded as a 'sissy.'"* —Stella Hay Rex, *Practical Hooked Rugs,* 1949

Chapter 2

Rug Hooking Terminology

A few words or terms are unique to rug hooking. Some are regional, found in certain areas of the country or in certain rug hooking communities and not in others. Some are different words for the same thing.

Allover. A freestyle hooking technique that fills large areas in a rug background by using squiggly lines or repetitive curlicues. Alternative names for this type of hooking include *higgledy-piggledy, annagogglin, antigoglin, bundling,* and *meandering.*

Backing. See *foundation.*

Carding strips. The sharp metal teeth in the strips that hold the backing taut on rug hooking frames. Carding strips are often the cause of rug rash.

Cat's paw. A basic bull's-eye shape with a small triangle of color in the center surrounded by concentric circular rows of different colors. Also known as *millefleur.* It can represent a flower or just be used as a pattern repeat.

cat's paw ~ mille fleurs

Cut. Referring to the width of a strip of wool. In general, strips are wide cut or fine cut. Patterns may call for narrow #3-cut wool or wider #8-cut wool. See chapter 9 for more information on cuts of wool.

Dummy board. A solid backing cut from wood or similar material and used to support a hooked piece. The wood is cut to fit the outline of the pattern. Popular subjects for dummy boards are people, pets, and especially Santa Claus. Dummy boards are often used for fireplace display pieces.

Fingering. A method of incorporating two or more different values or colors together. The blending process involves using interlocking strips of wool that are gradually turned sideways to fit two strips side by side and make the blending more subtle.

Foundation. The fabric into which the loops are hooked most often burlap or linen. Sometimes referred to as backing.

Holiday. An empty space in the rug, usually unintentional; a few missed holes.

Hooker. The jokes are endless, and you've probably heard them all. Use your imagination. See *stripper*.

Lamb's ears, Lamb's tongue. Decorative U-shaped flaps of wool stitched around the edges of rugs or

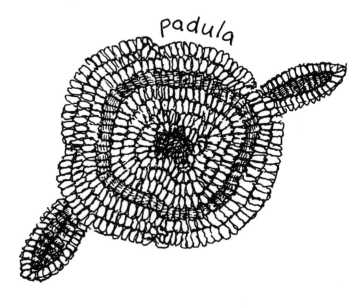

padula

mats for decorative effect. They are often layered like penny rugs and decoratively stitched. The tongue shape is also a hooked motif used within a rug or as a border.

Mat. Another word for a hooked rug; commonly used in Canada.

Motif. An element that is the focus of the rug or repeated often in the design: for example, a flower.

Needle felting. A craft entailing the use of a fabric backing such as wool or even denim, into which colored roving is pressed by the use of a barbed needle, called a felting needle. Multiple-needle tools make the felting process go more quickly.

Noodles. Leftover cut wool strips. See *worms*.

"Oh, shit." Commonly overheard in rug hooking groups, usually when a rug hooker has discovered that she's been using the wrong color, has twisted her strips, has run out of the color wool she needs the most, or has contracted rug rash.

Padula, pedula. The general term for a flower form that is ambiguous or imaginary; not taken directly from any specific type of flower.

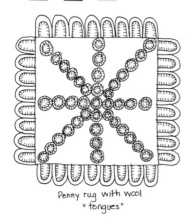

Penny rug with wool
"tongues"

stacked pennies for penny rug

Pennies. Concentric circles cut out of wool and layered atop a traditionally black wool background to create patterns. The resulting rugs are called penny rugs. The pennies are usually sewn in place with a blanket stitch for decoration. Also used as a motif or design element in hooked rugs.

Poison. The use of a color that seems incongruous to the color scheme of the rug; a bit of color that acts as a contrast or visual stimulus in the color scheme. For example, in a rug design that has a cool color scheme like blues and greens, a small area of a contrasting color, like orange or red, will be the poison. It will create movement and add a spark of visual interest.

Proddy. A rug hooking technique that involves pulling or pushing wide-cut wool strips from the back of the foundation to the front, giving a rough shag appearance.

Punch hooking. A style of rug hooking in which a special tool with a wooden handle and long metal shaft with a hole in the end is used to push the yarn into a backing, forming loops. Punch hooked rugs are hooked from the back of the pattern while hooked pieces are worked from the top or front of the backing.

Reverse hooking. A term with multiple meanings. In contemporary hooking, primarily in the United States, reverse hooking is a tongue-in-cheek term for pulling out the hooking that you've already done, usually in error. In Canada, reverse hooking is the technique of turning the rug over and hooking the loops from the back to create an area of lower loops for a special effect on the front.

Ribbon candy. A term describing how the hooking should look in a cross section of a row. The loops should form even up-and-down lines like the candy of the same name.

ribbon candy

Rug rash. The unsightly and painful scrape found usually on bared forearms of rug hookers. Rug rash is caused by dragging one's arm across the scratchy metal teeth of rug grippers or carding strips on the frame. See *"Oh, shit."*

Snippet. The trimmed-off end of a wool strip. Snippets congregate under the frame, on the floor, and around the borders of rugs being hooked, as well as make appearances in nearby water glasses and coffee mugs. On the practical side, snippets can be collected in containers and used for stuffing projects like small pillows.

Stash. The rug hooker's supply of wool. Like quilters, rug hookers have wool set aside from dyeing lessons and experiments and from special shopping trips to rug camps and the thrift store. Having wool on hand makes color planning easier because the colors are right there to choose from. The popular phrase is, "She who dies with the biggest wool stash wins."

Stripper. Of course it means the machine that cuts the wool into strips. However, when combined with *hooker*, it takes on a new meaning.

Thrums. See *worms*.

Turnovers. Not the delicious fruit pastry, but rather the point at which hooked leaves twist, showing the front and the back.

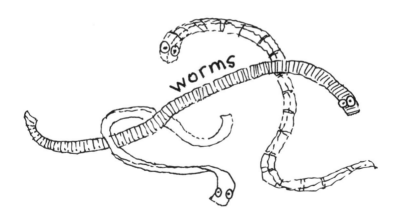

Worms, worm bag. A collection of wool strips left over from rug hooking projects. They are used for hit-or-miss rugs or as a source for small spots of color to add interest. A well-stocked worm bag is a great source for materials for small projects. Also called *gizzards*, *thrums*, or *noodles*.

Chapter 3

Types of Hooked Rugs

Hooked rugs come in all shapes, sizes, and types. These definitions will help you to determine what category your rug fits into, if any.

Aubusson

This French-influenced design style features a center design, usually floral, that is surrounded by patterned borders.

Azeri

This Oriental-style rug tells a personal story, usually about the hooker, through the depiction of objects or scenes in the hooker's experience. The background is often hooked in straight lines. The influence is from northeast Turkey and the Azeri and Kurdish tribes people.

Cheticamp

This Canadian-style hooked rug is from a region of Nova Scotia. The rugs are hooked with yarn rather than wool strips and are hooked low to the backing. The Cheticamp rug makers were organized by an

geometric

artistic designer, Lillian Burke, in the mid 1920s and then began selling their rugs. The business flourished into the 1950s when it was spun off by Flora Boudreau, who continues a rug hooking business in Cape Breton, Nova Scotia, Canada, in the Cheticamp style.

Cheticamp rug themes include pictorial historical scenes, religious imagery, and portraits in muted color schemes.

Crewel

A design style based on English embroidery patterns with an influence of old designs from India, crewel rugs feature elaborate flowers and bright colors, often referred to as Jacobean colors.

Geometric

A geometric rug design is created using shapes like squares, triangles, rectangles, and circles. Geometric rugs span a broad spectrum of design in many variations. Quilt patterns are a common geometric influence in rug hooking with the adaptation of popular designs like Log Cabin, Cathedral Window, Wedding Ring, and more.

Grenfell Rugs, Grenfell Mission

The Grenfell Mission was a medical and religious foundation started in the late 1800s by Sir Wilfred Grenfell. It was located in St. Anthony, Newfoundland and Labrador, and was designed to aid the poor.

Rug makers at the Grenfell Mission used Mrs. Grenfell's designs and designs of their own creation to make their rugs, which were sold to other hospitals and missions in the United States and Britain to earn money.

Motifs common to the Grenfell rugs include oysters, fish, polar bears, and other elements native to that area. The rugs were hooked with recycled materials like stripped jerseys and nylons donated to the mission. The rugs can still be found in private collections and are highly prized by collectors.

Hit or Miss, Hit and Miss

This general term describes a rug making process in which colored wool strips are pulled randomly from the rug hooker's bag of leftovers from other projects (see worms in chapter 2). The rug is then made from alternating colors from this mixed bag of strips.

The typical hit-or-miss rug is a geometric, featuring a wide variety of colors, textures, shades, and tones, hooked in straight lines or circles. The hit-or-miss name implies that the colors are picked blindly, but often the colors are grouped to make pleasing patterns or repeats.

Kilim

This Turkish-style rug design was traditionally woven from hemp, cotton, and wool. Kilim is a pile-less textile produced by one of several flat-weave techniques which originated in Turkey, the Balkans, Iran, Pakistan, and Afghanistan. Primary pattern motifs that are reproduced in hooked rugs are geometrics, including medallions, interwoven diamonds, and octagons.

Latch Hook Rugs

Latch hook rugs are different from traditional hooked wool rugs in a number of ways. They are made by pulling and knotting short, pre-cut lengths of colored yarn with a special hook through a large-opening, evenweave canvas. The process creates a fluffy, loose pile surface. Designs for the patterns are either drawn or printed directly onto the canvas backing, or the pattern is graphed on paper separately. The graph is followed by rows or by blocks of areas until the surface is completely filled in.

Often when discussing "rug hooking" with people who are not familiar with the technique of traditional rug hooking, they will comment that "I used to do that with kits when I was a kid!" At this point, rug hookers politely reply that what they probably used to do as a child was latch hooking.

Lunenberg

This precise form of hooking is practiced in Lunenberg County, Nova Scotia. The rugs were hooked primarily as geometrics, but the technique is what now defines the Lunenberg style. The rows were hooked with loops in every other hole, in alternating rows, so that the loops all lined up in both directions. Perfection was the goal.

Nantucket

The rugs defined as Nantucket style are originally from the New England coastal region and were popularized by Claire Murray. These rugs are hooked with yarn and without a frame. The work in progress is held across the lap with both sides tucked under one's legs and the yarn is pulled through the backing from the center. They most often depict nautical themes such as lighthouses, mermaids, and sea creatures, but include a variety of floral patterns as well. Most of the florals are hooked in pastels, often on dark backgrounds as a foil for the lighter colors.

Oriental

The Oriental rug is a style that follows design elements found in Eastern/Asian woven or tied rugs. The hooked Oriental rugs are created in both wide and fine cuts and feature geometric patterning in borders and backgrounds hooked in straight lines. The motifs often tell a story or display a scene. Colors are mottled or variegated.

Pictorial

As the name suggests, pictorial rugs tell a story, show a setting, illustrate a location, or create a portrait. Pictorial rugs range in cuts and styles from very realistic fine cuts with shading to simple stylized interpretations.

Portrait

Portrait rugs are also considered pictorial rugs, but the portrait style isolates or separates the subject and highlights it. Portrait rugs might be of people or animals and are created in a variety of styles, from realistic photographic reproductions to highly stylized interpretations with more vivid colors and abstract representation.

Primitive

This style is related to naive or folk art styles of rugs. Primitive rugs reflect a simplistic style with traditional elements and are rendered in minimal fashion. Motifs are flat, like cutouts. Colors tend to be dulled and unshaded. The scale and perspective of theme elements can be deliberately distorted to convey a sense of whimsy. Design elements in primitive rugs are often outlined with a dark solid line and filled in with a single color.

Materials used include recycled or alternative materials like denim or cotton fabric in addition to wool. Wool is often dyed to have a faded or splotchy appearance to duplicate the look of old rugs. Backgrounds are often random patches of color.

Proddy

Proddy tool

The term proddy refers to a type of rug technique that involves pulling and pushing $1/2$"-wide pieces of wool strips that measure 2" in length through an evenweave

primitive

backing. The colored strips are pushed through the holes using a specific tool that looks like an awl or a pointed pincher. The proddy work is done from the back of the foundation and the ends of the wool are pulled out to the front. Sometimes they are trimmed and shaped to form flower petals, but they can also be pulled up and left untrimmed, giving the rug a thick, shag surface.

prodded wool flower

Proddy creates a unique texture and becomes very heavy and sturdy.

Stained Glass

This name describes a style of rug that is created with dark outlines in a framework that resembles the leading in stained glass windows. Elements of stained glass are often religious themes, but not always. Any design can be modified in the style of stained glass. Blotchy colors are chosen to depict the mottled look of stained glass.

Tapestry

These rugs are created to mimic the fine woven style of wool wall hangings. They are created with very fine cuts and shading, and include traditional tapestry themes like the "Unicorn in Captivity" hooking pattern designed by Pearl McGown or works by the Morris design groups of the Craftsman era.

Three Dimensional

Rug hooking is not just for mats or rugs. There are many ways to create useful and fun items using hooked pieces. Three-dimensional objects like pillows, tea cozies, and

hooked purse

purses, and garments like vests and jackets all can be made from hooked material.

Traditional

This style refers to rugs created using dyed color swatches in graduated values and dip-dyed wool for gradual changes in color. The theme elements in traditional rug hooking include elaborate florals, scrolls, fruit, and medallions. A well-known designer of traditional rug patterns is Pearl McGown.

Waldoboro

This style of rug hooking is named for the New England town where it was developed. The sculpted wool technique allows design elements, like flowers for example, to be hooked in elevated rows, from lower on the outer edge to higher on the inside. The hooking is dense and close, and scissors are used to clip and trim the loops to form a smooth, rounded shape. These raised areas are incorporated into a basic rug hooking design with traditional level loops.

Chapter 4

Rug Hooking Tools

Starting a new venture is tricky. As we pick up a new craft, we want to have the necessary tools to work with, but we don't want to invest a large amount of money up front. Luckily, rug hooking can be as expensive or as inexpensive as you want it to be. Beginners can start off with basic supplies on a trial basis and add more expensive tools as they become more skilled and involved. The trick is to not get discouraged with cheaper tools in the beginning.

Basic Rug Hooking Tools & Materials

- Hook
- Frame
- Backing or foundation material with pattern drawn on
- Sharp scissors
- Yardstick
- Black permanent marker
- Masking tape

If you are creating your own pattern, you'll need the following:

- Photo or drawing of subject
- Tracing paper
- Pencil and eraser
- Light box or window to outside light source

Basic Tools

You'll need the following basic tools to start a rug hooking project.

The Hook

Rug hooks, the tool actually used to pull loops through the foundation material, come in many variations. The primary parts are simple: a metal shank with a hook at one end and a handle at the other. The variations are in the shape, size, and design of these elements.

Straight hook. This standard hook has a steel shank approximately 1" to 2" long.

Bent hook. The shaft is fixed at an angle for easier pulling.

If you are transferring a pattern to your backing, you'll need the following:

■ Red Dot or Blue Grid interfacing material

Bent Hook

Wide shank. The metal shank is fatter to widen the hole as it goes through the backing.

Trigger hook. The wooden handle is shaped like a gun handle to allow the hand more flexibility. This version is commonly chosen by those with arthritic hands to alleviate cramping.

Pencil hook. The long, narrow-bodied hook is the same size as a pencil. The handle is made of steel or wood and generally has a small shank and hook. It is used most commonly for fine cuts but is acceptable for wider cuts as well. Hold it as you would a pencil.

Ball hook. This hook has a small, rounded wooden handle with a shorter shank. The shanks on ball hooks vary; some are wide and others are not. The ball of the handle can be held in the palm of the hand or outside the hand in the space between the thumb and forefinger.

Crochet hook. The regular crochet hook itself works well enough, but the thin handle is not comfortable for long periods of hooking. It's not a practical choice in the long run.

The Frame

Frames also run the gamut of design and shape. The basic elements of a frame include a flat hooking surface with a way to fasten the backing to it so it fits snugly and doesn't shift. Some frames employ a series of nails over which the backing is stretched and then tightened by twisting the frame sides. Other frames have rug stripping, also called carding strips, which are a series of sharp fine teeth that are mounted on sturdy rubber strips and angled slightly away from the frame opening to secure the backing. Another frame design has the rug stripping with a set of wood paddles under the inside edge of the frame that snap tightly to hold the backing snugly.

Round hoop frame. The most basic frame is a round hoop, like a quilting hoop. For small projects, the round hoop can secure the backing so the rug hooker is able to pull the wool strips up from underneath.

The disadvantage of the round hoop frame is that it has to be supported without your hands so that your hands are free to do the hooking. Try resting the top edge of the hoop against a table or balancing it on one leg. Some hoop frames come mounted on legs and a base.

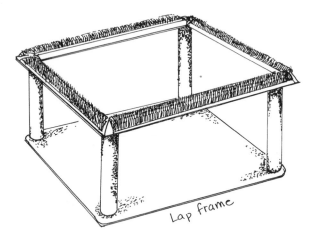

Lap frame

Lap frame. Lap frames are designed to sit in your lap. The basic design has a rectangular top with four legs and a flat surface for the bottom. Variations include a top that is angled slightly for greater accessibility or a top that is designed to swivel or turn.

Some small lap frames have a wooden tongue at the base for the rug hooker to sit on, making the frame more stable and freeing hands to hook. Others are designed to collapse and fold up for travel.

Floor frames. These frames are designed to be freestanding units. Essentially, a lap frame is mounted on a stand under which the rug hooker's legs fit, creating a working surface that frees up the hands. Many floor frames can be folded up in some manner for transportation, and some have fittings for trays and lights, making a handy workspace.

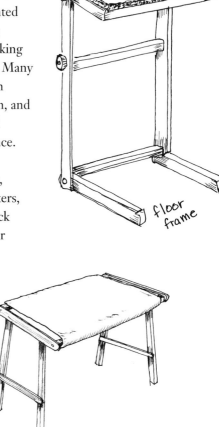

floor frame

Frame free. Some rug hookers, notably the Nantucket rug makers, hook without a frame. They tuck both ends of their pattern under their thighs and work the area in their lap, pulling the yarn up from underneath, between their knees.

Caution: Be careful about how you move your arms across the surface of the frames with rug gripper strips, as they can be scratchy. See *rug rash* in chapter 2.

Cheticamp-style frame

The Scissors

In the pursuit of keeping costs at a minimum, beginners can use standard scissors to trim the wool strips, but specialty scissors make the task much simpler.

Whatever style you choose, the best scissors are those that are sharp. Dull blades will mangle the ends of the strips. Also, choose scissors that fit your hand comfortably. Scissors that are too long or too small for you will cause a strain on your fingers and hands. Try several styles for comfort—you'll be using them a lot.

Small embroidery scissors or snips. These will do the job well enough. The key to using small scissors is to remember that the trimmed tails of the wool strips on top should all be cut evenly with the surface of the loops. When trimming ends, pull the tail up, tug on it slightly, snip it off, and allow it to tuck neatly between the loops. This procedure requires that you hold the scissors parallel to the surface of the rug.

curved embroidery scissors

Bent scissors: Angled in a Z shape with the cutting edges parallel to the surface and room for the handles above the surface, these scissors work very well to keep the trimmed ends even.

Bent or Offset scissors

Cutters

Cutters are used to cut large pieces of wool into strips to be hooked. They can be either hand cranked or electrically powered. See chapter 9 for more details.

what better place for
a pet to sleep?

"'Can you use moth-eaten clothes?' is a common question. Yes, indeed. The moth is a loyal friend of the rug hooker. He sends many a good woolen garment our way. Indeed, we have even been accused of maintaining our own private army of moths to invade the closets of our friends."
—Stella Hay Rex, *Practical Hooked Rugs*, 1949

Chapter 5

Patterns

A pattern is the basic design for a rug, drawn on the backing in a way that gives a clear definition of what is to be hooked. Patterns can be traced onto the background, or printed, silk screened, or drawn with a stencil. Paper patterns can be copied or traced onto the foundation material (see chapter 6).

Paper Patterns, Patterns, and Kits

Rug designers offer a variety of combinations for rug hookers. These are some of the options:

1. Paper patterns. The design is drawn on paper, either to the exact size or smaller to be enlarged by the user. Some designers draw the pattern on a transfer material like tracing paper or red dot interfacing.

2. Pattern on backing. The design is drawn or printed onto the foundation fabric, which can be linen, burlap, monk's cloth, or rug warp. Sometimes the patterns are packaged with a photo of the finished rug.

3. Kit. The designer assembles a package that includes a pattern on backing, directions, and the wool needed to complete the project. Some kits come with the wool already stripped, while others supply the wool uncut.

When purchasing patterns, make sure they are drawn or printed squarely onto the backing. Check the outer lines to be certain they are lined up in the groove of the linen and that the border lines do not skip or cross over rows. Many a rug hooker didn't realize that her rug was out of square until the lion's share of the work was completed—and by then it's too late.

— linen
backing

Pattern drawn off the grain

Commercial patterns are available from a wide variety of sources. In addition to established shops, hundreds of rug hooking artists create and sell their own patterns. Check online or contact a rug hooking group like ATHA or *Rug Hooking* magazine (see chapter 16).

Drawing Your Own Patterns

Drawing your own patterns is not as intimidating as you might think. With the proper tools, you can draw up your own pattern from scratch and create your rug from the ground up.

There are some important things to consider, however. If you are going to draw a design of your own creation, totally out of your own head, more power to you. But sometimes you want to use a source that is not from your own imagination, be it a photograph, painting, book illustration, magazine article, and so on. If you are using any other source, you must seek permission and you must credit the original.

Copying someone else's work is a huge no-no. One bandied-about rule states that changing the design by 15%, or some other magical percentage, will make it legitimate, but this is not true. If you use a source that is not your own, then give credit where credit is due, and in the case of wanting to use someone else's material, get permission in writing.

It seems awkward, but if you explain what you want to do, most of the original source owners are happy to allow it. Be respectful of their rights and give them credit on the back of the rug in your label or identification tag.

The following basic elements are covered in an article from *Rug Hooking* magazine, Vol. XV, 2003, in an article by Jennifer A Ryan, Esq.

Copyright. Copyright is a written protection for the work of writers, artists, designers, or photographers. It is a legal form of protecting the creator from having his or her designs copied or reproduced without permission. The standard length of protection of work is the lifetime of the artist or creator plus 70 years.

Original pattern/design. Any design that has unique elements that have not been previously published or displayed is considered original. While some basic elements like common shapes or items in and of themselves are not protected by copyright, combinations of these items may be original to that artist and protected by copyright.

Protected items: Anything with the copyright symbol is protected. A general rule for judging whether or not an image or design is protected is to calculate the time it was created. Items created prior to 1923 are no longer protected, and items after 1923 still are.

It is illegal to photocopy a design and transfer it for your own use without permission of the designer. For example, you may not copy a pattern that a friend has purchased and use it.

Fair Use Doctrine: This law allows you a certain limited amount of usage of a design or part of a design for specific purposes. It protects the creator of the design from having multiple copies of her work duplicated and sold without her knowledge or permission.

What it boils down to is this: Do not copy other people's designs. Buy and use patterns or draw your own without copying the work of someone else.

In order to protect your own original work, you must register your design with the Copyright Office of the United States Government. Go to *www.copyright.gov*, click on "How to Register a Work," then print out the forms to be filed under "Visual Arts."

bundle of joy

Chapter 6

Backings and Foundations

Traditional rugs were hooked into burlap backing or feed sacks and flour sacks. Burlap patterns are still available today, but most patterns are drawn on other foundations. Let's take a look at modern foundations, how much you'll need, and how to transfer a pattern to the backing.

Modern Foundations

Today rug hookers use a variety of foundations, or backings, for their rugs. Burlap is sometimes still used today, but it has several drawbacks: strong smell, uneven threads/not square, deterioration over time/drying out, fuzzy texture, airborne fiber, slubs, and flaws in the threads. The following commonly used foundations eliminate some of these flaws.

Linen evenweave. Linen is a natural fabric made from flax fibers: strong, with no chemicals, and long lasting. It is available in different weave counts and comes in bleached (light color) or unbleached (tan or brown color) options. It has a very firm surface. Note: Watch for the amount of "hairs," or fibers, that stand up from the surface. Some types of linens are considered to be less hairy, and therefore fewer stray bits of the white foundation fibers pop up between the loops.

Rug warp. This cotton weave fabric is softer and heavier than linen. It also has smaller openings in the weave. Most rug hookers find it better for small cuts of wool.

Monk's cloth. This cotton weave cloth has a looser tension. It is suitable for different cuts of wool and offers a flexible surface.

Scottish burlap. This higher grade of burlap is more evenly woven and bleached to soften the texture and color. It has fewer "hairs" than other burlap.

How Much Foundation Do I Need?

Figure out the image size for your rug. For example, let's say you want the main body of the rug to be 16" by 20". If you want to add a border, let's say a 2" border, then you need to add a total of 4" to account for the border on each side.

$$16 \times 20$$
$$+ \ 4 \ +4$$
$$\overline{20 \times 24}$$

Now add some working room, let's say 3" around, so you have to add 6" more:

$$20 \times 24$$
$$+ \ 6 \ +6$$
$$\overline{26 \times 30}$$

This is the outside measurement of the fabric that you will cut from the bolt. Use a yardstick on a flat surface to measure out this size on your backing, then draw a line with a permanent marker to indicate that outside edge.

To block off the main parts of your rug, measure 3" from each outside edge for your working area. Draw the lines with the marker.

Then measure 2" inside that line to give you a 2" border and the final body area for your design.

Transferring Your Design to the Foundation

Several methods are available to transfer your design to the foundation you'll be hooking into. There is no "right way"; there is only the way that works best for you.

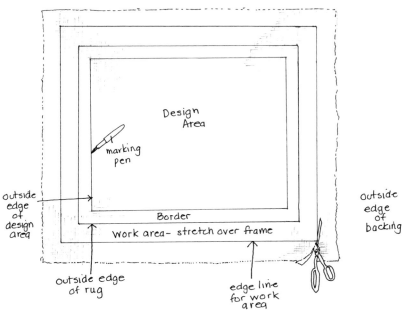

Design Area

marking pen

outside edge of design area

Border

Work area- stretch over frame

outside edge of backing

outside edge of rug

edge line for work area

Sizing a rug

Freehand. The most basic method of transfer is to draw a pattern freehand onto the backing material.

Tracing. This technique allows you to copy the design drawn on a separate piece of paper. Use a light box for the source of light, or tape the drawing to a window and then tape the backing over the drawing. The underlying design will show through the backing. Trace the lines with a marker.

Red Dot/Blue Grid. This process involves using a fabric transfer material that is used as interfacing in sewing. The semi-translucent material is printed with either small red dots at 1" intervals or with a 1" grid printed in fine blue lines.

This material can be laid over the drawing or photo source, traced, and then placed over the backing material. Once it's in place, use a marker to go over the outlines of the design on the Red Dot or Blue Grid material. The magic marker penetrates the transfer fabric.

Tape the screen over the drawing

and trace it with a marker

Red Dot and Blue Grid interfacing are available in fabric stores and online.

Screen. This technique uses standard screen door material as the transfer medium. Found in hardware stores, the screen stock is sold in rolls. Look for vinyl gray screen, not the metal or the black vinyl.

Simply lay the screen, cut to size, over the drawing or pattern you wish to transfer, make a tracing onto it with magic marker, then lay the screen over your backing and trace over the lines of the pattern.

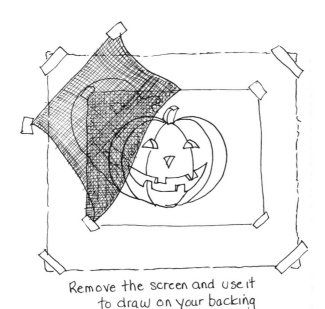

Remove the screen and use it
to draw on your backing

The marker will pass through the holes of the screen onto the backing material.

With the screen and the Red Dot/Blue Grid transfer methods, you have a permanent, reusable pattern for making more than one rug of the same pattern.

"To man or woman, maker or observer, seller or buyer, but perhaps especially the maker, a hooked rug will open up hitherto unrealized vistas in the mind. Speculation on the principles behind the design, the properties of the plants or dyes which provided the color, the ways of combining the colors, the psychological sense of well-being in creative activity, identification with the sturdy early folk whose background enters into the entire tradition, are all phases which combine to make this activity as fruitful as it is satisfying." —Estelle H. Ries, *American Rugs,* 1950

Chapter 7

Accessories

Like any other art, rug hooking can be done with a minimum of tools. However, a few accessories do make rug hooking easier, quicker, and more fun.

Cutter stands. Some rug hooking cutters are designed to clamp onto the edge of a table, which works well to secure them. However, sometimes a table is not available or the edge is too wide to accommodate the clamp. Fortunately, you can find stands designed to hold the cutter by itself. These stands are available from some of the cutter designers themselves or made independently by artisans using their own designs.

Rug frame covers. These handmade fabric covers are designed to provide protection of and from the metal teeth of the rug grippers on the rug hooking frame. They are available on websites and at specialty stores that sell rug hooking tools.

snippet holder

Snippet holder. Sure, you can use an empty cup or scrap of a napkin to collect your trimmed ends of wool, but why not be classy about it? Snippet holders include a wide variety of cups, mugs, bags or pockets designed to sit on or near the rug hooker's frame and keep the litter of wool bits to a minimum.

Oops! wrong container...

Scissors fob. Fobs are decorative chains, handles, or clips designed to attach to your scissors so you can keep track of them while you are hooking. Some scissor fobs come with clips to fasten to the front of a shirt; others have hooks to attach the scissors to the rug hooking frame. You'll find a variety of styles and types, many decorative or stylized.

Magnets. Pairs of small magnets can be sewn into fabric covers and used to provide a grab-spot on the tightened rug backing on the frame. One magnet on the top of the backing and one underneath will give a moveable place to set scissors safely as you hook.

Chapter 8

Wool: the Paint on Our Canvas

Wool is the product of sheep's fleece, combed and spun and woven into fabric. Wool has been produced for centuries for garments and bedding, upholstery and carpeting. It is durable, warm, and versatile.

Wool is wonderful for making rugs because it is flexible, sturdy, strong, and stain-resistant with superior colorfastness. It is naturally fire retardant, durable, and lasts for many years. With proper care, wool rugs can last for generations, and what better way to create a memorable heirloom than with such a beautiful material?

For rug hooking, wool is the fabric of choice, but rug making is not limited to wool fabric alone. Rugs can be hooked with yarn, cotton fabric, paisley fabric, denim, jersey fabric, and basically any material flexible and strong enough to be pulled through linen. There are even rugs made from plastic bags!

Finding Wool

So where do we find wool for making rugs? You can purchase yardage off the bolt from a mill; buy it from a rug hooking store or business that specializes in dyed wool; or reuse wool garments from thrift stores, garage sales, or even Grandma's closet.

"Upcycling" Wool

Recycling is not a new term or process, and much has been done to reuse and recreate new materials from old and discarded ones. But upcycling is a new word for taking unused or previously used materials and producing something of greater value from them.

Hooking rugs from scrap materials is a centuries-old tradition, born of necessity and ingenuity. But it's important to keep old traditions relevant and current, so categorizing our use of hand-me-down wool or old paisley or even plastic bread bags as "upcycling" makes a statement that not only is rug hooking a significant process of creating heirloom art, it's part of an environmental and positive modern movement.

Mills

Only a few fabric mills are left in the United States, as most of the work is done outside the country.

However, if you are interested in buying yardage in a variety of traditional textures, colors, and weaves, then mill wool off the bolt is a good way to go. It is consistent in color and texture and can be dyed, stripped, and hooked reliably.

Woolen mills serve a variety of purposes, from selling finished wool goods, clothing, and wool fabric to offering services for carding, spinning, and dyeing wool. Some mills are sheep farms with a sideline in wool. The best way to find out if they offer wool fabric for rug hooking is to contact them.

Shops and Online Stores

A handful of stores sell rug hooking supplies and wool, but they are not usually large national chain stores. Contact rug hookers in your area for information about local shops, or contact guilds for where to buy wool.

Rug hooking supply businesses are easy to find online. You'll find large companies and mills that sell materials and wool online and ship them to you, as well as small, privately run home businesses that dye wool and sell it along with other rug hooking supplies. Use a search engine to find one you like and contact them about their policies for shipping and returns.

Thrift Stores

The thrill of the chase! Going to a thrift store in search of wool is exciting and fun—you never know just what you might find. Myriad sources of wool abound: suits, skirts, blazers, slacks, and blankets are usually for sale at very low prices. You will be dismantling the garments, so be sure that you have a stitch ripper and sharp snip scissors in your stash of tools at home to make the task easier.

Kilt. The prized piece is the kilt, which when snipped at the seams reveals almost a yard of pleated wool that can be pressed and used with very little extra effort. It is the crown jewel of thrift wool.

Skirts. Skirts are bounties of wool fabric, with a little more effort than kilts. Look for the largest sizes and check the label for the Woolmark logo, which means it is certified as 100% pure wool. Feel free to experiment with wool/polyester blends, but keep in mind that they may not hook as easily as pure wool.

Suits. Wool suits are often made from wool called serge, which is thinner and has less body. It's not the best to hook with because it is thin and wimpy and doesn't fill the holes in the backing as well as heavier wool. It is useable, in a pinch.

WOOLMARK

Blazers. Wool blazers seem like a lot of fabric, but you may need to decide if they're worth the extra effort of cutting apart the back, sides, arms, lining, and collar. The actual yield of usable wool can be less than skirts provide.

Slacks. Slacks are good for long pieces of wool. There is a work factor with them as well because you'll be removing hems, zippers, pockets, and waistbands.

Coats and blankets. Coats and blankets are usually made of heavier weight wool. They may provide useable wool, but consider what you will be using them for. If they are too heavy to strip up and yank through linen backing, perhaps they would be better to use as a backing or as appliqué or penny rug material.

There is one rule of thumb for bringing home wool from thrift shops or garage sales: Keep it separated from other fabric until it has been washed. Some rug hookers bring wool home in a plastic bag and put it in the freezer until they have time to wash it. This practice prevents the spread of moths or larvae that could be hidden in the garments, as well as potential smells from a house with a smoker or pets.

Washing wool from garments is tricky, but it's a step you don't want to skip. You can either wash the garment first in its entirety and then dismantle it, or you can take it apart and wash the pieces.

If you wash it first, select a delicate setting on the washing machine and choose a cool/warm temperature setting. Don't overheat or over-agitate the wool. Both heat and agitation cause wool to shrink, and you can expect to lose generally an inch or two overall to shrinkage. Use a small amount of mild detergent to eliminate odors and bugs.

When the garment is finished in the washing machine, take it out and either dry it on a line or in the dryer. Again, choose a delicate setting and low to cool heat, and throw in a large bath towel to help absorb and distribute the moisture. Do not over-dry the wool pieces.

When the wool is dry, take your scissors and seam ripper and get to work. Take off the waistband, buttons, and zipper, and undo the hem stitching. Tear out the lining, open up the seams, and snip any pleats or darts. Dismantle the pockets.

When the garment is in pieces, fold and store it in a cool, dry place, like a plastic storage tub or a clean, lined shelf.

Wool in Its Many Forms

For rug hookers, wool is the lifeblood of our work. We choose wool for color, texture, and durability, and when we are finished with our rug, we have created a piece of art that should last for generations to come.

Textured Wool. Wool can be woven in the most basic, flat texture in neutral or natural colors. It can also be woven into textures, which include the following:

herringbone

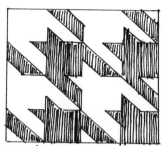

houndstooth

stripes

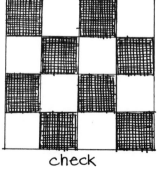

check

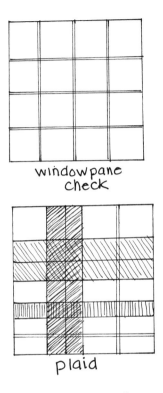

windowpane
check

plaid

These textures are dyed in endless varieties of color, give life and body to rug designs, and make an interesting visual palette for the rug hooking artist.

Felted Wool. Not to be confused with wool felt, felted wool is wool that in a washing process has been overheated or overagitated to the point of extreme shrinkage. The felting process condenses the fibers of the wool and creates a matted material that is too thick to be used for hooking. It can still be used as a sturdy backing or for other types of projects.

Wool Felt. Wool felt is a product of wetting loose wool fibers and binding them together to form a fabric. Wool felt is commonly sold in craft and hobby stores, in cut squares. Because it is not sturdy or stable enough to be pulled through a linen backing, wool felt is not useful for rug hooking. It is best used in piece form for appliqué.

Roving. Combed wool fleece yields a soft, fluffy material known as roving. Roving can be spun into yarn on a spinning wheel, but it can also be used in this fluffy form for needle felting work. (See Needle Felting in chapter 17.) Rug hookers can use roving to add an interesting element: using the felting needle, the colorful fibers can be integrated into the hooked wool to create fine lines of contrast and texture.

Yarn. Yarn is not only made from sheep's wool, it can also be spun from other animal fleeces like alpacas, llamas, and goats. The long skeins of yarn are created by spinning flax or roving into long twisted fibers that form the yarn.

Some yarns are a blend of wool and acrylic fibers. The acrylic yarns are durable and can be used in rug making, but some lack the feel or texture of real wool.

Yarns have many practical applications in the rug hooking world. Rugs can be hooked using yarn instead of wool strips in a process called punch hooking (see chapter 17).

Yarn can be used to whip the binding of a rug in the finishing process and provides a type of bumper around the edge, which protects the hooked edges. It can be dyed to match the colors in a rug.

You Have the Wool; Now What?

Wool fabric has its own vocabulary, which is used in rug hooking in similar ways to the terms used in the sewing world. Here are some key words to know when it comes to using wool.

Grain, on the grain. The weave of the fabric. The straight lines formed by the weaving of the threads both lengthwise and crosswise show the grain of the fabric. It is important that wool strips be cut on the grain to keep the integrity of the weave even, as off-grain strips will shred, tear, or not lie flat in hooking. If there is still a selvage edge on the fabric, use that to determine the grain, which is parallel to the selvage. Generally, a piece of wool fabric will tear more easily on the straight grain.

Flannel weight. The generally accepted weight of wool used for rug hooking, which equates to about three quarters of a pound per yard of fabric. Coat or blanket wool is heavier; suiting wool is lighter weight.

Notches. Markings added by the seller. Wool sellers will often dye yardage of wool and sell it in half-yard pieces. If they choose to sell portions of these half-yard pieces, they cut or tear a small notch every sixteenth yard or so to indicate both the measurement of the wool as well as where the selvage was, allowing the user to keep a straight edge.

Pure wool. Denotes no other materials/fabrics were used. Using 100% wool to hook your rugs is best whenever possible because of the consistency and durability of the weave. Some element of synthetic or polyester fiber is still acceptable; however, be aware of how it affects the dyeing or cutting of the wool blend.

When shopping the thrift shops or garage sales for wool garments, look for the familiar triad of wool circles to indicate 100% wool.

Selvage, selvedge. The finished woven edge of the wool as taken off the bolt. The selvage runs along the top and bottom of the wool fabric lengthwise and is denser and more tightly woven than the rest of the fabric. It finishes the edge.

Solids. Any single-colored wool. See *texture*.

Tearing, ripping. In order to keep a straight edge without going off the grain of the weave, it's best to square up or straighten your piece of wool by tearing with the grain. Once that line is torn, you can follow the threads to cut straight, even strips.

Texture. In rug hooking this term refers to the woven pattern of the wool. It creates visual contrast more so than a tactile contrast. The textured wools include plaid, houndstooth, tweed, and herringbones, while the wools without woven patterns are considered solids.

How Much Wool Do I Need?

This can be tricky, because most rug hookers do a guess/estimate of the wool they need for a project based on the area of the rug times a factor of five or six. A common way of figuring out if you have enough wool is to lay the rug pattern out, take a piece of wool that is folded five or six times, and lay it over the area to be hooked. If it covers the drawn part of the pattern, then it will probably be enough to hook that section.

Of course, every rug hooker uses wool differently. Sometimes, if they "hook high" with loops pulled up farther than average, they will use more wool. Or if they "hook tight" with the loops packed together, they will use more wool. These tendencies should all be factored in when deciding how much wool will be needed for a project. Fine cuts tend to use more wool as well. Dip-dyed pieces are often cherry-picked for specific areas of color on a piece, which can affect coverage because only portions of the strip are used.

If there is one rule to hooking that needs to be followed, it is to always have more wool than you think you will need. If you dye your own wool, you can at least go back and dye more if you run out, but if you are working from a limited stash, you can find yourself short. And that is not a good thing.

> *"Whenever my mother would start a rug, my father would say, 'Well, Mother's got a mat in the frame—now we'll not get anything to eat.'"*—Stella Hay Rex, Practical Hooked Rugs, 1949

Chapter 9

Wool Strips

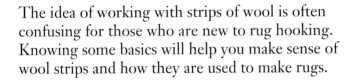

The idea of working with strips of wool is often confusing for those who are new to rug hooking. Knowing some basics will help you make sense of wool strips and how they are used to make rugs.

Understanding Cut

The cut refers to the width of the wool strip. Cuts are different sizes, and they are categorized in groups. These include fine cut, which are the narrowest widths, from #2 through #4 or 5, and wide cut, which

The number associated with a width size is based on $1/32''$.

#2 = $1/16''$

#3 = $3/32''$

#4 = $4/32'' = 1/8''$

#5 = $5/32''$

#6 = $6/32'' = 3/16''$

#7 = $7/32''$

#8 = $8/32'' = 1/4''$

#8.5 = $5/16''$

#9 = $6/16'' = 3/8''$

#9.5 = $7/16''$

#10 = $8/16'' = 1/2''$

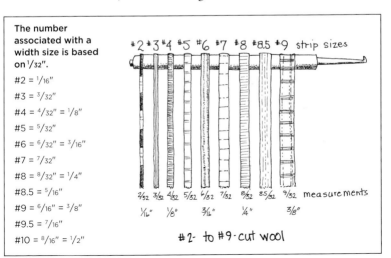

#2 #3 #4 #5 #6 #7 #8 #8.5 #9 strip sizes

$2/32$ $3/32$ $4/32$ $5/32$ $6/32$ $7/32$ $8/32$ $8.5/32$ $9/32$ measurements

$1/16''$ $1/8''$ $3/16''$ $1/4''$ $3/8''$

#2- to #9- cut wool

includes #6 to 9. Wide cut is also known as primitive cut. (Primitives are wide cut, but not all wide cuts are primitives. See chapter 3.)

Cutting the Wool Strips

Rug hookers have options for cutting their wool into strips, and those options vary from relatively inexpensive to fairly expensive. A rug hooker can spend as little or as much as he or she chooses for this process. Beginners just getting started may decide to cut by hand at first then graduate to more expensive tools later, or stay with the least expensive method and let it go at that.

Cutting by hand with scissors. Bare bones expenditure would be a pair of sharp scissors or shears. Many rug hookers cut their wool strips by hand, eyeballing the width, and are satisfied with the variations in width from strip to strip. The by-hand cutting technique works better with wider cuts of wool, but many rug hookers have taken scissors to strips to cut the narrowest strip of wool to fit a certain purpose.

Cutting with a rotary cutter, mat, and ruler. The next step up from cutting strips by hand is to use tools familiar to the quilt community: a rotary cutter, a self-healing mat, and a wide, see-through ruler.

Using the mat, which is usually printed in 1" increments like a ruler, a rug hooker can get pretty consistent results for evenly cut strips.

The mat and rotary cutter tools are easily stored and transported and are relatively inexpensive. It's easy to cut a variety of sizes of wool strips in a speedy process.

Cutting with a machine designed specifically for wool cutting. Once you feel committed to making rugs, you may decide to invest in a more specialized cutter. A variety of these cutters are available from different manufacturers, and they can be found in rug hooking venues like shops and online vendors.

A wool stripping machine is cuts multiple, uniformly sized strips of wool easily and consistently with minimum effort. You feed a piece of wool into the cutter and turn a handle or crank that pulls the wool through a series of blades, cutting the strips to specific sizes. Some machines are even electric, operated with a foot pedal.

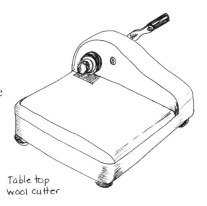

Table top wool cutter

Rigby. This table-mounted wool stripper features interchangeable blades. It uses a crank handle and attaches to the table edge with a clamp. It requires a wrench to change the blades for different sizes of cuts. Made in the USA.

Bliss. These machines, made by the Fraser Rug Company, are table-top cutters with interchangeable blades. The Model 500-1 uses a clamp to attach to the edge of a table. The Model A is engineered to cover the cutter gear section and has suction cup feet to attach it to flat surfaces. The Model A cuts up to $1/4$" strips. These machines also use a wrench to change cutter blades. Made in the USA.

Honeydoo. These wool strippers are freestanding units with a carrying handle cut out at the top. There are two models: the Blue Devil and the Red Racer. The Blue Devil has a hand crank, and the Red Racer is electric, run with a foot pedal like a sewing machine. They offer three cutting heads from $2/32$" to $16/32$". Made in the USA.

Bolivar. This hand-cranked cutter clamps to the edge of a table with a built-in set screw. The Standard model has three shear heads that are not interchangeable or removable. They cut three different strip widths. The Triple Base Model V has the same basic design as the Standard, but shear heads are interchangeable and can be swapped out using the provided tool. The Single Base Model V is the same as the Triple Base, but holds one shear head at a time. It's lighter and smaller than the other models. Made in Canada.

Bee Line-Townsend. The Townsend cutter is crank operated and clamps onto the table edge. It is fitted with interchangeable blades set in cutter heads, or cartridges, which are available in $3/32$" up through $1/2$". They offer an extension device called a Kitmaker, which allows a wider cutting base to cut more strips at one time. The new Townsend cutter is designed and sold as the Bee Line-Townsend Cutter. Made in the USA.

"A hooker who had received as a gift a quantity of good woolen underwear spent the entire morning dyeing it for an autumn-leaf rug. A neighbor, coming home for lunch and spying the garments on the line in all their gorgeous crimson, yellow, and orange hues, called excitedly to his wife, 'Margaret, for God's sake come here and see the underwear the Grants are wearing!'" —Stella Hay Rex, *Practical Hooked Rugs,* 1949

Chapter 10

Playing with Color

Rug hooking, as with many forms of art, relies on color as part of its definition. Even monochromatic rugs are defined by the values and contrasts we see on the gray scale.

Color Wheel

In rug design, a color wheel is used to show the relationship between colors. The color wheel was first created by Sir Isaac Newton in 1666, and while modifications have been made, the basic concept is the same. The wheel is composed of three primary colors, three secondary colors, and all degrees of color in between.

Another version of the color wheel was created by Professor Albert H. Munsell. This color system was designed to place colors into a three-dimensional form, like a globe of variations in color based on hue, value, and chroma. Munsell was not able to make the perfect sphere, and instead developed the scale into a series of stacked circular arcs. He based the system on a gray scale of 10 neutral values from 1 (black) to 10 (white).

Munsell's color wheel did not include the secondary color of orange, so his wheel was composed of five colors instead of the six on Newton's wheel. They both included the primary colors of red, yellow, and blue, and the secondary colors of green and violet. Munsell dropped orange because it occupied less space on the color spectrum.

Classic rug hooking teacher Pearl McGown used the Munsell color system for her rug hooking color planning. A detailed description of the color process can be found in her 1954 book, *Color in Hooked Rugs.*

The color wheel is a simple method of viewing the relationship between the colors and their many combinations.

Primary. A color—red, yellow, or blue—that yields other colors when mixed.

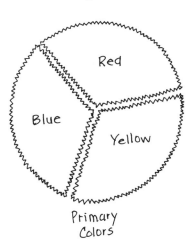

Primary Colors

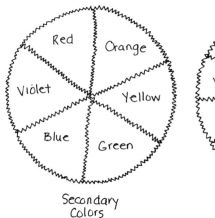

Secondary
Colors

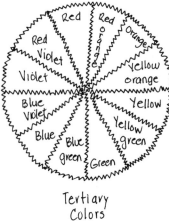

Tertiary
Colors

Secondary. A color—orange, green, or violet—that is produced by mixing two primary colors.

Tertiary. The colors formed by mixing a primary and a secondary color: yellow/orange, yellow/green, red/orange, red/violet, blue/violet, blue/green.

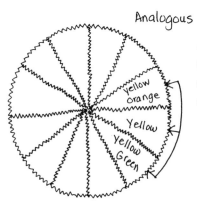

Analogous

Analogous. Three colors on the twelve-hue color wheel that are side-by-side: red, red/orange, and orange, for example.

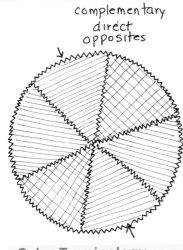

complementary
direct
opposites

Complementary. Any two colors on the color wheel that are directly opposite each other; red/green, yellow/violet, and blue/orange are examples of complementary primary and secondary color complements.

Color Terminology

Advancing colors. Warm colors that tend to come forward visually in a composition, expanding.

Chroma. Purity of color, or the absence of white or gray in it.

Color. The quality of an object with respect to light reflected by the object, usually determined visually by measurement of hue, saturation, and brightness of the reflected light.

Contrast. The relative difference between the intensity of light and dark elements in a composition.

Cool colors. Colors in the color wheel in the purple, blue, and green range.

Gray scale. A range of achromatic colors having several (usually 10) equal gradations ranging from black to white.

Hue. Color; gradation or variation of a color.

Intensity. The strength of color due to the absence of mixture with its complement.

Receding colors. Cool colors that tend to contract or shrink visually in a composition.

Saturation. The degree of chroma, or purity of color, based on the absence of white.

Shade. The degree of darkness of a color determined by the quantity of black or a complement.

Tint. The degree of lightness of a color, a color diluted with white, and of less than maximum purity or saturation.

Value. The second dimension of color; the element of lightness or darkness.

Warm colors. The colors in the color wheel that include yellow, orange, and red.

Chapter 11

Your Dyeing Day

Dyeing wool seems like a scary undertaking, but there are many benefits. For one thing, you control how much wool you need as well as the types of colors you create. This control saves time and money in the long run, and prevents waste. There's nothing wrong with having a stash of wool waiting to be used, and there's a lot to be said for having the ability to make what you need when you need it.

You'll find many techniques for dyeing wool and a lot of terminology. Start with one source and one technique, get a feel for the process, then experiment with other techniques and processes. Dye books are useful guides to the different dye techniques, and they provide basic dyeing information as well as recipes for specific colors. Once you have a handle on the basics, you will find that dyeing is not only fun, it's also practical and often addictive.

Tools for Dyeing

A plethora of small, mostly inexpensive items make up the basic tools required for most dyeing techniques. Specific techniques may require

Basic Dyeing Materials

- Apron
- Heavy duty rubber gloves
- Colander
- Cotton mask
- Tongs
- Enamel or stainless steel pots: 12 qt. to 16 qt.
- Enamel, glass, or stainless steel roasting pan
- Glass measuring cups (1 cup and 2 cup)
- Wide mouth glass jars (1 quart)
- Measuring dye spoons
- Wooden or other long-handled spoons
- Plain salt (noniodized)
- White vinegar
- Synthrapol or Ivory liquid dish detergent
- Dyes
- Scissors
- Notebook and pen
- Whisk, for stirring dyes

long handle tongs

white enamel dye pot

additional items, like rubber bands for tie-dye. Most of these items are available at grocery or hardware stores, but items like the dye spoons and Synthrapol must be ordered from rug hooking specialty shops or online.

Several companies manufacture powdered dyes for wool. The acid dyes are created specifically for

single measure

dye spoons

glass measuring
cup

dual measure dye spoon

Powdered Acid
Dye Packet

Powdered Acid Dye
Jar

animal or protein products like wool, silk, or nylon.

Be sure to store your dyes and your dyeing tools
away from young children and your cooking utensils.
Dye is not a toy, and you don't want to confuse your
dye pot with your spaghetti pot!

Dye Vocabulary

Acid dye. A type of dye formulated for use with animal products such as wool or silk.

Agent. See *wetting agent*.

As-is wool. Wool that is original in color and texture, not re-dyed. Also called "off the bolt."

Citric acid. A chemical agent used to set the dye after it has been absorbed into the wool (see *mordant*).

Dye bath. The water and dye solution combined in the dye pot to dye wool pieces.

Dye solution. The specific measurement of dye to the amount of water into which it is dissolved. Usually in a one cup measure.

Dye spoons. Special spoons made to measure dry dye; available in increments from 1 teaspoon to $1/128$ teaspoon.

Formula. The recipe for combining dye colors.

Hand-dyed. Wool that is dyed by an individual rather than commercially.

Drink mix dye. Powdered drink mix used as a dye; results are usually very subtle and may not be stable; fades.

Mordant. A chemical agent that fixes or sets the dye color in the wool during the dyeing process (see *citric acid* and *vinegar*).

Natural dye. Colors created by using plant forms like berries, leaves, and grasses. For example, onion skins and walnut shells are two types of natural dye sources.

Pre-soak. Allowing wool to soak in water prior to dyeing; may include adding a wetting agent (like Synthrapol or Ivory liquid dish detergent or Wetter than Wet) to make it easier for the wool to absorb the dye.

Swatch. A strip or strips of wool dyed in graduated color values.

Synthrapol. A liquid chemical wetting agent added to the water in which the wool soaks prior to dyeing.

Union dyes. Powdered dyes that are combined with salts.

Vegetable dyes. Dyes made to be used with plant fiber, like cotton, rather than with wool; for example, Rit brand dye, which is used for cotton rather than wool, may still work with wool but lacks stability or intensity.

Vinegar. Used as a mordant, or agent, to set dye color in the dyeing process.

Wetting agent. A chemical product added to the water in which the wool soaks prior to dyeing; the agent allows water to permeate the fiber, making it easier for the dye to be absorbed.

Dye Processes

Abrash. A dye method of using multiple colors on one piece of wool, mostly in Oriental rugs.

Antique black. Wool with a black base and a green or brown cast to make it look old or faded with use.

Bulk dyeing. Adjusting basic dye formulas to accommodate larger amounts of wool being dyed at one time.

Casserole dyeing. Gathering wet wool to be dyed in folds and placing it in a shallow casserole dish, then spooning dyes across the surface.

Crock-pot dyeing. Using a crock-pot to heat the water and dye the wool; makes small amounts.

Dip dyeing. A traditional dye technique in which strips of wool are dipped in stages into the dye to create a light to dark gradation in color on each strip.

Gradation dyeing. A dye process that creates a series of wool strips in a progression of color values.

Dip dye
single strip

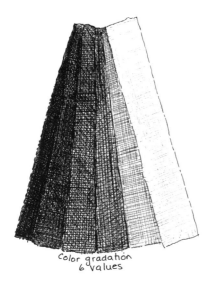

Color gradation
6 values

Jar dyeing. A method of dyeing using six to eight glass jars seated in a large roasting pan filled with water; dyes in the jars span a light to dark range of color, allowing you to achieve a full line of gradation in one process.

Marbleizing. Rolling two or more dyed pieces of wool together and simmering them in water to create striated color bands as the colors mix between pieces. Usually done without adding any dye.

Marrying. Combining wools of different colors and simmering them together to allow both colors to mix, creating a similarity of color between the two. You may add another soft color to make the blend smoother.

Mottled. An uneven, blotchy surface achieved by not stirring the wool during the dye process so the color is not evenly distributed; creates a visual texture.

Onion skin. Using the papery skins of onions to make a dye; boiling the skins and using the liquid creates a reddish brown color.

Open pan dyeing. Using wool in a single pot to achieve one color.

Over dyeing. Wool that has already been dyed or colored at some point is dyed again to change the color or enhance it.

Painted dyeing. Using a brush to apply the placement of the dyes on a wet, flat piece of wool.

Scrunch. Using a smaller pan to condense the wool and give it a mottled, variegated surface as dye pools in the deeper nooks and folds.

Spot dye. A dye technique in which the dye is applied in separated areas in spots or blotches, usually alternating two colors or more.

Tie dye. Gathering together sections of the wool in rubber bands or string, then applying the dyes around the area, creating bursts of color when the bands are untied.

Trans color dye. A process of creating bands of color in a specific planned order on a single piece of wool.

> *"There is joy in work; and to create a thing of beauty ourselves or to help others to express their idea of things that are to them lovely and of good repute is, to put it mildly, soul satisfying."* —Anne M. Laise Phillips, *Hooked Rugs and How to Make Them,* 1925

A BASIC DYE PROCESS

This bare bones discussion of a simple dye process is only presented to give an idea of the essential steps of what dyeing entails. For every step listed here, there will be another version—or twenty—in other sources. My advice is to choose one method to start, master it, then expand your knowledge.

1. Gather materials and prepare a cleared area in which to work. If you're dyeing in a kitchen, cover all surfaces with newspaper to protect against spills.

• • • • • • • • • • • • • • •

2. Tear or cut the wool to the required sizes, usually 1/2 or 1/4 yard, as described in the formula or recipe you're using. Getting the correct size is critical because formulas are based on specific sizes of wool. Smaller pieces will yield a darker color saturation; larger pieces will yield a lighter color.

• • • • • • • • • • • • • • •

3. Fill a large container with warm water and a few drops of a wetting agent like Ivory liquid soap or Synthrapol to help the water penetrate the deepest fibers of the wool fabric. If possible, soak the wool overnight to guarantee saturation. Note: If you're in a hurry, a minimum of a couple of hours can suffice, as long as the wool is thoroughly soaked.

• • • • • • • • • • • • • • •

4. Boil water in a small pan or kettle. This water will be poured into the dry dye to dissolve it.

• • • • • • • • • • • • • • •

5. Fill dye pots with water, about two-thirds full. Turn up heat to bring the water to a boil. This water will be used for the dye baths.

• • • • • • • • • • • • • • •

6. Put on rubber gloves and a cotton mask. Measure out the dry dyes with special spoons according to the recipe. Some recipes require that you mix your dry dyes together in one mixing cup and add boiling water; others have you dissolve individual colors in separate cups and blend them in the dye pot.

• • • • • • • • • • • • • • •

7. Pour the boiling water into the measuring cup, then stir the dye with a whisk until it is completely dissolved.

• • • • • • • • • • • • • • •

8. Pour the mixed dye solution into the dye pot; this is now the dye bath. Recipes will tell you the water/dye ratio. They vary from recipe to recipe.

• • • • • • • • • • • • • • •

9. Mix with large spoon to distribute the dye throughout the water.

• • • • • • • • • • • • • • •

10. Take the pre-soaked wool out of its container, gently squeeze out the excess water, and add the wool to the dye bath.

• • • • • • • • • • • • • •

11. Use the large spoon to move the wool through the dye. Frequent stirring yields a more evenly colored piece of wool; scarce stirring allows the dye to settle unevenly for a more variegated finish.

• • • • • • • • • • • • • •

12. Reduce the heat to medium and let wool absorb the dye. Note: Certain colors are absorbed quickly while others are slow to soak in. Don't be discouraged if it is going slowly—wait until all of the dye has been absorbed.

• • • • • • • • • • • • • •

13. After about half an hour, add a mordant such as white vinegar or citric acid. The mordant will cause the water to clear as the last bit of dye is taken into the fabric. Stir to ensure that the mordant is distributed and keep the heat low until the water is clear.

• • • • • • • • • • • • • •

14. After the water is clear, or mostly clear, remove the pot from the stove. Carefully pour off the water through a large colander; let the wool drop into the colander.

• • • • • • • • • • • • • •

15. Allow the wool to drain.

• • • • • • • • • • • • • •

16. Rinse the wool in clear hot water, gradually cooling the temperature until it's lukewarm. Alternately, let the wool cool to room temperature and use the delicate cycle on a washing machine without soap with warm/cool water.

• • • • • • • • • • • • • •

17. Hang the rinsed wool outside or on a drying rack. Alternately, put the dyed wool into the dryer on the delicate setting and add a large clean towel to lower the static buildup and catch extra fuzz.

• • • • • • • • • • • • • •

18. Be careful not to cool the wool too quickly or drastically (like plunging it into cold water) or it will draw up and become felted.

• • • • • • • • • • • • • •

19. Clean up the mess.

Chapter 12

Filling the Empty Spaces

Rug hookers use a wide variety of techniques to fill the spaces of their patterns. Try any one of these favorites for some variety.

Beading. A technique that uses two contrasting colors of wool strips pulled up alternately to create a line that looks like beads on a necklace or an inlay in wood furniture. The process involves holding both strips with your fingers under the surface and pulling the colors up in alternating order.

Contour. The line that defines the shape of an object; an outline. In rug hooking, it can be a solid line in a color that contrasts against the color of the object for definition.

Directional line. The process of using a line that creates movement diagonally or wavy lines instead of straight lines. When hooking areas that could be simply flat looking, this technique gives the composition a sense of movement.

Echo. The technique of hooking a series of rows that expand outward from a motif or design element like

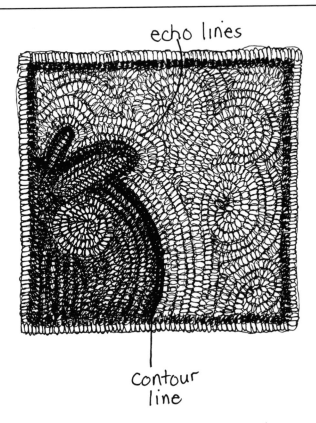

echo lines

contour
line

ripples on the surface of a pond. This is a good way
to fill in a background space.

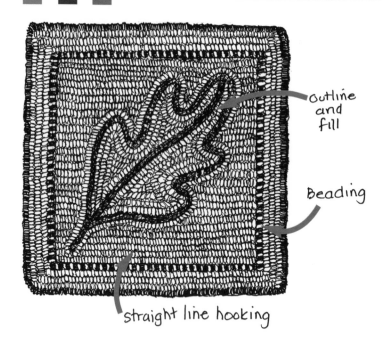

outline
and
fill

beading

straight line hooking

Filling in. Hooking an outline of a motif or area and then filling in the empty space. Filling in becomes more interesting if the hooking is done to follow the inside edges into the center of the area or hooked in directional lines inside the area.

Straight line. Filling in an area by hooking in the lines of the backing in rows. This technique lends a sense of calm or stability to backgrounds. Straight lines can be hooked horizontally or vertically in the composition. Also called "in the ditch."

Chapter 13

The Big Finish

You've done it. The hooking is complete and your rug is ready to be finished. Finishing has several steps: steaming or pressing the rug, binding the edges, and attaching a label.

Steaming and Pressing

Sometimes in the hooking process the backing draws up or becomes distorted due to the tension of the wool being pulled through the holes. Especially when hooking concentric circles, a dome-like area can form. In any case, pressing or steaming the rug is always a good idea before attaching the binding. This process squares up the edges and eases the tense sections of wool to allow the rug to lie flat.

To steam or press, you will need an iron and a flat, firm surface on which to lay the rug. Make sure the surface is not sensitive to heat or moisture. Place a dense, absorbent pad down (a terry cloth towel works well), then lay the rug on top of it, face down.

Dampen a cotton cloth, like a sheet or a towel, and lay it on top of the rug. Start in the middle of the rug, press the iron down evenly, hold, and then lift the iron. Move the iron to an adjacent space, press, lift. Do not push or rub the iron across the surface; just apply smooth up-and-down pressure. Problem areas can be pressed more than once, and it may take more than one pressing over the entire rug to make it lie flat. You can re-dampen areas that still have bulges and press them again.

Binding Techniques

Rugs need to have a finished edge in order to protect the loops around the outside edge and to provide a safety bumper against wear and tear. If a rug is going to be used on a floor, the finished edge will keep the corners and sides of the rug safe from the stresses of foot traffic.

Different binding techniques are designed to both give the rug an attractive finish and protect it from wear and tear.

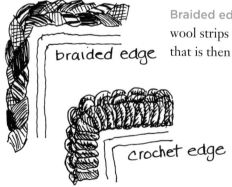

braided edge

crochet edge

Braided edge. A process using wool strips to make a heavy braid that is then attached to the finished edge of the rug.

Crocheted edge. A more decorative way to finish off the edge of the rug. One attractive finish combines whipping and crochet: first whip the edge with wool, then use wool strips or yarn and a crochet hook to crochet another edge around the rug.

Knotted fringe. Yarn is cut to a specific length and knotted through the whipped yarn edge to make an even trim.

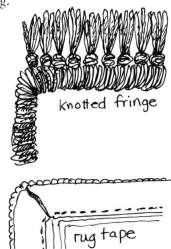

knotted fringe

Rug tape. In this binding process, lengths of cotton tape are stitched to the back, outside edge of the pattern before the hooking begins. The tape defines the edge and allows you to hook as close to the sides as possible. When the hooking is completed, the binding is tacked down to the back of the linen for a smooth, clean finish.

rug tape

Twisted rope. Yarn is entwined/twisted together to form a rope, which is then attached to the edge of the hooking.

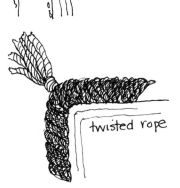

twisted rope

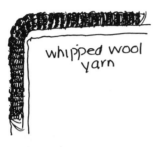

whipped wool yarn

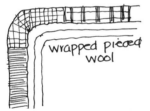

wrapped pieced wool

Whipped edge. A process requiring yarn as a finishing medium. When the hooking is completed, excess backing material is trimmed within an inch or so from the hooked edge. The excess backing is then either folded to form an edge or turned over a cotton cord. In both techniques, use long straight pins to secure the rolled or folded edges until they can be basted, if desired, and then whipped.

Heavy yarn, preferably wool yarn, is then whipped over the rounded edge, forming an even, smooth bumper all around the rug. Thinner yarn can be doubled to make a thick edging.

Or use cut wool strips to whip the edges to form a binding. They should overlap slightly to cover the binding all around.

Wool-covered cord edge. A process in which a cotton cord is encased in a long strip of wool and sewn to the back and edges of the rug, giving a smooth, even edge.

SPECIAL FINISHING CONSIDERATIONS

The design of the product, especially if it's three-dimensional, will define how it's to be finished. Purses need handles and a lining; pillows need to be backed with fabric (if you're not using two sides of hooked material) and stuffed, and may have decorative edges like beaded fringe or cording. Garments like vests need to be stitched together and lined, hemmed, and fitted. Tea cozies may require a lining for insulation.

hooked tea cozy

hooked purse

hooked coasters

Labels

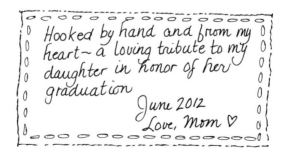

Rug Title
Designer
Hooked by
Date completed
Rug dimension
Cut/strip size
Material used
Backing
Notes

Label for
back of rug

This critical finishing touch is often overlooked by many rug hookers. It's important to label your work because it gives credit and identification to a piece you have created. Beyond that, a label is an identifier for future generations. And in a practical sense, a label is a requirement if the rug is to be entered and shown in exhibits or rug shows.

Your rug label doesn't have to be expensive or elaborate. Commercial labels are available in a variety of formats, but you can simply cut out a small piece of cotton fabric, trim the edges with pinking shears to

Hooked by hand and from my
heart~ a loving tribute to my
daughter in honor of her
graduation
June 2012
Love, Mom ♡

prevent unraveling (or serge or zigzag them), then write the information in indelible ink.

It is also a good idea to include any interesting information about the piece, especially if the design is original or if the rug was created as a gift. Consider writing a personal note to the recipient or signing your name. Your rug is a historic creation and should be labeled as such.

When you've completed the label, loosely tack it to the back of the rug with a needle and thread or use a safe iron-on adhesive.

Basic Label Elements

- Name of the rug
- Name of the artist who designed it
- Name of the person who hooked it
- Date it was completed
- Dimensions
- Cut (width of strips) used
- Material used: wool, wool yarn, etc.
- Type of backing or foundation

"The owner of practical hooked rugs has no need to wince when she sees them walked upon. She realizes that with each step they are being worn to a softness of shading and texture that will make them choice heirlooms someday."
—Stella Hay Rex, *Practical Hooked Rugs,* 1949

Chapter 14

Care and Display of Hooked Wool Rugs

Once you've hooked and finished your rug, you'll need to follow some basic principles dictating how to care for your hooked rug. Whether you hang it, display it on a table, or use it on the floor, certain precautions will prolong the life and beauty of your hooked piece.

■ Avoid using rugs on the floor where there's a lot of traffic. They survive longer and will be admired more easily if they are off the busy footpaths of your home, resting in bedrooms or in less busy parts of the living or dining room.

■ Don't hang rugs or display them in direct sunlight. Even though the dyes are colorfast, continued exposure to sunlight will fade them.

■ Keep the back side open and free to "breathe." Lift the rug off the floor regularly and air it outside to freshen the wool. Never apply a rubberized coating to the back or enclose it with a solid sewn lining. Both will cause the wool and the foundation to deteriorate.

If you choose to hang the rug, be sure that the hooks distribute the weight of the rug evenly. If you hang it with brads (short headless nails), secure it across the upper edge with the nails evenly spaced and not straining the backing.

If you use self-fastening tape, or Velcro, then stitch the positive side to the rug with heavy thread and attach the negative side to a wood lath strip that can be mounted to the wall.

You can also sew a fabric pocket like a curtain rod pocket to the back of the top of the rug and run a flat piece of wood lath through it, then hang the encased rod on the wall over evenly spaced nails.

Storage

Rugs must be stored with great care to prevent damage and unwanted deterioration.

Make sure the piece is free from dirt or debris, hair, and loose fibers.

Roll it up gently *with the hooked side out* to avoid putting extra strain on the linen foundation.

- Never fold a hooked rug. The strain along the rows can cause permanent separation along the fold.

- Never wrap the rug in plastic. Moisture can become trapped inside and cause the wool to mold or mildew. Instead, wrap it in a clean white cotton sheet or pillowcase.

- Do not store wool rugs where temperature can fluctuate to extremes. Basements can be damp and cold and attics can be dry and hot, so store the rug in an area of moderate climate.

Cleaning

Hooked rugs have been around for hundreds of years and most of the old ones were used on the floor, proving that they are both durable and long-lasting when given proper care and attention. Some modern hooked rugs never see the floor, resting comfortably on tabletops or hanging on the wall like fine art, as well they should!

But at some point, if you find that your hooked rug has become soiled, you will have to clean it.

- Dirt. Use a brush attachment from your sweeper to gently sweep across the surface, but don't use a beater-brush vacuum cleaner as it can pull the loops out of the backing, ruining both your rug and your vacuum.

■ Isolated spills. Dab these gently without forcing the offending liquid or particles deeper into the loops.

■ Stains. Using Woolite or Ivory liquid dish detergent in very small amounts, create a foam by briskly stirring the cleaner in water, then apply small amounts of the foam to the stained area. Use a soft brush to sweep away the foam. It's a good idea to do a test spot on the back of the rug to check the wool for colorfastness.

■ General all-over dinginess. One of the old tried-and-true methods of cleaning hooked rugs calls for winter weather. Take the rug outside, shake it to loosen any bits of dirt or debris, and then lay it front side down in granular, clean snow. Do not allow the rug to become soaked, but gently press it against the surface of the snow, then lift it and move it to another clean patch. After the dirt has been loosened, brush the rug carefully with a whisk broom and then drape the rug face up on a flat surface to dry.

No matter how bad the stain looks, do not immerse a hooked rug in water and never soak the foundation or backing. It is difficult to dry the rug completely, and the moisture and subsequent drying could loosen the structure that holds the loops in place and eventually cause rot. Seek a rug cleaning professional if you're out of options.

Moths, Ugh

Moths cause a lot of damage for such small critters, but with preventative care and attention, you can keep them out of your wool stash and your rugs.

Moths are the adult stage of the insect, and they don't eat wool. But when they are in the larval stage, they can eat holes galore. The best way to prevent the infestation is to make sure first that the area where your wool is stored is clean and free of old fabric, old shoes, or anything that would be a food source for moth larvae. Dust and sweep under furniture and vacuum drapes and wool carpeting in the areas where your wool will be stored.

Cedar has long been used as a moth repellent. You can buy small blocks or balls made from cedar to help repel the insects. Moth balls

clothes
moth

made from naphtolene are no longer in favor as they have a very strong chemical odor that is difficult to erase and may be harmful to humans. However, newer chemical products that kill and repel moths can be hung with wool garments. Some natural choices include lavender and dried orange peel with spices. These fragrant plants and fruits don't kill the moths, but they can repel them.

Restoration

The amount of damage and the area where the rug is damaged will determine the method of repair.

If loops have simply been pulled out, you can use your hook to pull them through the backing in their same holes or adjoining holes.

If the loops have been severed, it's possible to pull up loops using the pieces and butt the ends up against each other.

If strips of wool are missing completely, wool of a similar color and texture will have to be found or dyed as close to a match as possible.

If edging is worn or missing, then look for either wool or yarn to match the existing material. Trim away the damaged area and gradually work the new material into the edge where the damage was.

If there is a hole or tear in the rug, patch the backing with a similar material (burlap, linen, monk's cloth) by lining up the grid of the replacement backing with the damaged or missing area. Stitch the patch to the surrounding area, then hook in with matched wool strips.

Look for rug restorers who specialize in hooked rugs. You can find them online or in rug hooking publications.

Penny rug with wool "tongues"

Chapter 15

Inspire Me!

So let's say you want to create your own pattern. Anyone can do it. It's immensely satisfying to draw your very own pattern and hook it; an original rug takes on a certain depth of meaning and you have a personal feeling of accomplishment.

Some rug hookers, and not necessarily those who are beginners, are reluctant to draw up their own designs. It seems intimidating to those who don't have much experience in drawing to compose and lay out a rug design. Where do you even begin?

Every rug starts with an idea, a concept, a goal. Is the rug a gift for someone else? Is the rug a personal fulfillment of a dream? Is the rug going to reside in a specific place, like that empty spot on the kitchen floor or that blank area above the fireplace? Is the rug for practical use, or is it a decorative statement?

Start by deciding what the rug is to be used for. If it's going to a specific area, measure the area and be sure to leave adequate, balanced space for the rug when it's finished. You may not want to make a table runner that runs off the ends of the dining room table, for example, or make stair risers that don't fit the space of the stairs.

If the rug is a gift, make a list of requirements. Is this a wedding, birthday, or anniversary gift? If there is to be information included in the rug, like names and dates of the event, be sure that you have the information correct and spelled properly.

If you know the recipient, it's worth considering their color scheme and decor. Granted, a rug will probably outlast any one period of decorating colors and styles, but if the lucky recipient has contemporary tastes and likes bright colors, it might not be a good idea to hook a primitive style rug with muddy colors. Use your judgment, and consider to whom the rug will be given.

Sources of Inspiration

Now you have an idea of what you want to do, but you could use some inspiration, information, and a source for your drawing.

First, look at your own collection of photographs, both printed pictures and digital files. You can find some great ideas right in your own scrapbook or family album. Here are some ideas for rugs you could create from your own pictures:

- family tree rug
- homestead, family farm, grandparent's house
- portrait of family member or members
- weddings, anniversary parties, reunions
- pets, babies, children at play
- vacation spots
- famous landmarks, like the Grand Canyon or Yosemite or Broadway

Really, the sky's the limit. You not only create a wonderful rug, but preserve and celebrate a special moment from your own life. What better way to honor your heritage than with an heirloom rug?

If you want to go outside your own collection of photos, think about other sources of inspiration. Look at your flower gardens and take pictures of those beautiful roses, pansies, lilies, tulips, and irises when they're in full bloom. Look at garden catalogues for specific types of flowers. Observe how the leaves and petals look, what the colors are.

How about quilt patterns? Many rug hookers use them to make lovely rugs, including Double Wedding Ring, Log Cabin, Nine Patch and countless others. Pieced or appliquéd, quilt designs lend themselves to rug designs because they are simple and easy to do.

Men like rugs too, both hooking and receiving them. If you're making a rug for a guy, consider these options:

- sports: feature team colors, mascots, venues like famous stadiums or arenas
- hobbies: golf, hunting, fishing, sailing, etc.
- symbols or icons of occupations or military service

Remember to be respectful of copyrighted and trade-marked materials as your source. Photos, team logos, or insignia may be protected and cannot be copied.

Speaking of other sources, don't forget some simple ones that you may have around the house. When you are looking for inspiration, why not check out these:

- old Christmas cards and greeting cards
- children's picture books, nursery rhymes, coloring books
- greenhouse or flower gardening catalogues
- china and wallpaper patterns for border ideas
- quilt books

When you start developing your color palette, check paint stores or hardware stores for paint chip strips to help you choose the colorways for your rug. Do a small mockup of your pattern on tracing paper, and then color it in with colored pencils. Color outside the lines if you want to!

Chapter 16

A Learning Experience

■ ■ ■

Taking a class or workshop can be a wonderful experience that will enrich your rug hooking abilities and broaden your horizons. Not only will you learn something about any number of rug hooking techniques or skills, you will be surrounded by people who love rug hooking.

The class experience fosters motivation, inspiration, excitement, and creativity. You meet people outside of your usual daily experience and you learn from them, as they learn from you.

Here are some basic questions to consider as you choose a class or workshop:
- Is this a skill or topic I want to spend time and money to learn about?
- Is the teacher knowledgeable? Look at their history, their work, their biography.
- Is the class within my budget? Can I afford to travel there and stay there?
- What are the policies if I need to cancel?
- Do I have to buy a pattern or kit from the teacher, or may I bring my own?

Some teachers bring wool and items to sell at workshops. You are under no obligation to buy their products. For some students, a teacher's wool, books, and patterns may be their only access to such materials, so it is a good opportunity for them to buy wool for their stash and save the cost of shipping.

Look for classes, workshops, retreats, and camps in the ATHA magazine and *Rug Hooking* magazine. Both have comprehensive lists of events well in advance for you to choose from.

There are also listings online at individual teacher's websites and at the camps themselves.

When You Go

When you sign up for a class or workshop, read the information carefully. If you take a class that is too far beyond your abilities, you could slow down the progress of the class. There's nothing wrong with taking a class that challenges you, but jumping in too far over your head will cause resentment from your classmates and frustration for your teacher, who will have to give you extra attention.

You're paying to learn something, so go in with an open mind and willingness to learn. You're a student, not a teacher, and if you have an opinion or a criticism to share, save it for a private moment with the teacher. No one likes a know-it-all who disrupts the discussions or is disrespectful of the teacher.

Be respectful of your fellow students. Keep a tidy space and clean up after yourself; pick up loose wool strips and wool dust. If you borrow a tool from someone, return it promptly. Keep your discussions quiet and listen when the teacher is speaking.

Basic rug camp rule: be nice. Go with an open mind and you'll gain more than you ever expected.

What to Bring

Your teacher will probably give you a list of what you need, but there are some basics that most workshops require.

- frame
- hook(s)
- scissors
- notebook, pencil, pen
- Sharpie marker
- wool stripper, cutter
- favorite accessories: snippet holder, scissor fob, footstool, etc.

Rug Camp Buddies

Chapter 17

World of Woolcraft

You can use wool in many creative ways other than rug hooking: the applications and combinations of techniques are endless. With access to different types of wool and creative tools, artists can explore their creativity in countless ways. Some of these techniques can even be incorporated into your rug.

Wool Appliqué

In the process of wool appliqué, shapes are cut from wool fabric and stitched to a backing material, usually also wool. Shapes can then be adorned with

wool appliqué

fancy hand-stitching, beads, and other decorative application to enhance the design.

One popular type of wool appliqué is called a penny rug. [See chapter 2.]

Rug hookers also use the penny rug motif in their hooked rug designs, hooking different colored concentric rows to form circles.

Rug Punch Needle

The punch needle process for rug making involves using a wooden-handled

Oxford punch needle

hollow needle through which wool yarn or narrow wool strips are threaded, then punching the yarn to form loops in a sturdy fabric backing like linen. The designs are drawn onto the back of the rug and punched from the back so the loops appear on the front. The tool is designed to form loops of the same size for an evenly finished surface. The height of the loops can be adjusted on the needle.

Rug Punch Chair Pad

Needle felted Purse

Embroidery Punch Needle

The same idea behind rug punch needle is scaled down to make smaller, finer projects with an embroidery punch needle. The needle is smaller and uses embroidery floss or wool thread for the loops instead of thicker rug yarn. Instead of an evenweave linen for backing, this type of punch uses a tighter woven cotton fabric like weaver's cloth.

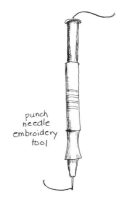

punch
needle
embroidery
tool

Like rug punch needle, the embroidery punch needle designs are also drawn on the back of the foundation fabric and punched from the back, forming small loops. Often the designs are small replicas of historic rugs and are used in dollhouses.

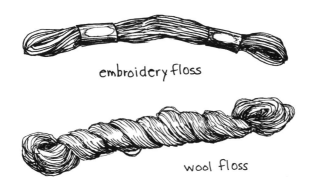

embroidery floss

wool floss

Needle Felting

single needle for
felting wool

This process is used to attach wool roving to a backing fabric using one or more needles to push the fibers of the roving into the backing. The roving is carded fleece that has been combed and dyed and has a fine, fluffy consistency. Under the backing fabric is a sponge or mat that will allow the barbed needle to pass in and out without breaking, causing the roving fibers to attach to the backing.

needle felting
tool
pen style

The needles have tiny barbs on one end that push the roving fiber into the weave of the backing material. Repeatedly pushing the roving into the backing holds the roving relatively secure. Any pattern
or design can be worked into a needle felted piece.

The needle felting process can also be used to create three-dimensional objects. By forming the roving over a basic structure or armature, the roving is built up in layers to make any number of shapes or forms.

ball of roving

needle felted
bunny

Chapter 18

Where Rug Hookers Flock

The rug hooking community is full of groups, guilds, and associations where rug hookers can go for information, education, and connections.

ATHA: Association of Traditional Hooking Artists

This nonprofit organization is an open guild of rug hookers—students, teachers, and distributors—all with the same goal: to stimulate interest in the art of traditional rug hooking, to share information and ideas about art and to promote educational activities that will upgrade and improve the quality of rug hooking. *www.atharugs.com*

Green Mountain Rug Hooking Guild

Located in Vermont, the Green Mountain guild is a source for information, education, and organization of rug hooking interests. They host "Hooked in the Mountains" consisting of a rug exhibition, workshops, and vendors at Shelburne Museum's Round Barn. *www.gmrhg.org*

Joan Moshimer's Rug Hooker Studio

Pattern designer and teacher's group, this website presents information and products. *www.wcushing.com*

Ontario Rug Hooking Guild

A network of over 1,000 textile artists with an annual exhibit each spring. They offer a certification program, workshops, and a rug registry. *www.ohcg.org*

Pearl McGown Hookrafters

Pearl McGown was a driving force for education, information, and distribution of rug hooking across the country. She established a system for certification of teachers, found sources for materials, and wrote books about color and design. *www.mcgownguild.com*

Rug Hooking Guild of Newfoundland and Labrador

A rug hooking guild based in Eastern Canada. They offer certified teachers, camps, hook-ins, and a variety of projects for guild participation. *www.rhgnl.ca*

The Rug Hooker's Network

An online source for all things rug hooking. *www.rughookersnetwork.com*

TIGHR: The International Guild of Handhooking Rugmakers

This group operates online as a source for rug hooking information, a group for making connections to other rug hookers internationally, and for project information. *www.tighr.net*

For more community opportunities, either in person or online, check out resources like *Rug Hooking* magazine, the *ATHA Newsletter*, and *Wool Street Journal*. Their articles are loaded with information about rug hooking as well as related arts.

The Internet provides a wide variety of information, and finding one source usually leads to many more.

"'Make it yourself!' is the best American tradition. To pioneer wives and mothers it was a necessity. If they wanted to brighten their rough cabins they had no other resources to rely on except their own energy and ingenuity. . . . For there is no satisfaction to equal that creative pleasure which comes from watching a fine piece of work grow from under your fingers." —Stella Hay Rex, *Practical Hooked Rugs*, 1949

As we embrace a new form of art, there is so much to learn. No one starts any type of new venture knowing all there is to know about it. What would be the fun in that? It's the learning process, the acquiring of the handling of the tools, the feel of the wool, the joy of exploring color and design. These are the elements that we grow with and learn from.

You are an artist! Whether you are creating a hooked piece from someone else's pattern or making a set of placemats, you are a creative force making something of value. The men and women who hooked rugs over the years probably never suspected that their humble handwork would be passed along through generations, but these are the pieces of history we can hold onto. These are heirlooms we create now, for our children to enjoy and pass along to their children.

The *Rug Hooker's Companion* was created as a tribute and an aid to those who love hooked rugs, those who admire and enjoy the feel of wool and love the blending of the colors as they merge and grow across the backing. I hope the knowledge shared here will be a help to both the beginner and the accomplished hooker.

And don't forget: You can never have too many friends, too much chocolate, or too much wool!

Appendices

Appendix I

A Rug Hooking Primer

So how does this rug hooking thing work?

First, you must collect your tools. You will need a frame, a hook, a pair of scissors, a pattern drawn on backing material, and stripped wool. Make sure you have a comfy seat and good lighting. Squinting and straining over your frame will take a toll on your eyes and your back.

floor frame

Stretch your pattern material on the frame, centering it over the open area. Make sure it's as snug and as even as possible, lining up the weave of the backing material with the sides of the frame. Some rug hookers leave some slack in the fabric, but to get the most even, consistent loops pulled, a taut and square surface is best.

Take your first strip of wool in the hand you don't write with and hold it under the surface of the backing. Hold the strip between your thumb and index finger like you're pinching it. Holding your hook in the hand you write with, gently push the hook into a hole in the backing just inside the drawn line of the pattern. Feed the end of the wool strip to the end of the hook, catch it, and pull it through the hole so the tail of the strip pops up through the surface, leaving about a quarter inch of the end sticking up.

Push the hook down through the hole next to the tail you've just pulled up, feed the strip to the hook with your fingers underneath the backing, and catch it with the hook, pulling up a loop that forms about one quarter inch above the surface. Release the loop off the hook, put the hook into the next hole and repeat, pulling up another loop next to the first one, keeping the loops the same height.

Skip the next hole and pull a loop into the one after that. If you hook every single hole, the wool will be too tightly crammed into the surface, which is called "packing." The surface of the rug will be drawn up by the tension of the loops and will not lie flat. Hooking too tightly also wastes wool because you use more than you need. Wool needs air to expand and contract naturally, so remember to space your loops evenly. You will develop a pattern of hooking— hole-hole-skip, hole-hole-skip. With practice, the wool will tell you where it needs to go.

At the end of your strip, pull the last bit of the tail to the surface. You should have a line of wool loops that runs evenly across the surface. From the side, the row should look like ribbon candy.

ribbon candy

To continue, take your next strip of wool, hold it under the surface next to the tail you just pulled up, and put the hook into the same hole you just pulled the tail through. Pull up the end of the new strip flat against the tail of the first strip, release it, then push the hook into the hole next to the two tails that are sticking up together and pull up a loop level to those in the first strip. Release the strip, reach and pull a loop in the hole next to it, release, skip a hole, and pull up a loop in the next hole. Continue to create hooked lines to form an outline of the area you're filling up, pulling up tails as you go. The loops should stand like a row of soldiers, shoulder to shoulder. They should not be zigzagging like a zipper or rolling up and down like a roller coaster. You can adjust the height of the loops by gently tugging the loops with the hook to even them out.

To start a second row next to the first row, leave a row of backing open and push your hook through the backing into a hole one row over. If you're carrying over from a previous row, you'll continue hooking right to left and left to right, back and forth, with an empty row between the lines of hooked wool strips. The backing will be able to expand and contract, to "breathe."

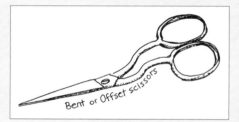
Bent or Offset scissors

Your tails will be sticking up slightly higher than the surface of the rug loops. Some hookers leave the tails standing without trimming them as they work across the surface; I trim them as I go, or in brief intervals of hooking. To trim a tail, tug it gently up, trim it across evenly, and release it. Don't cut at an angle. The slight tension and release will let the tail pull itself back just under the surface of the loops beside it, hiding it from view. The tails of your strips should not be higher than your loops.

Some basic tips for hooking:

Hook the outline of each area first and then fill it in. Hook just inside of the line, as hooking on the line or outside of it will distort the image. This is important on rugs with a geometric pattern or in rugs with fine detail. See the chapter for filling in to see how to direct your hooking lines.

When hooking circles, start with a series of loops in the center and hook concentric rows outward. Make sure to keep the rows evenly spaced because the backing can draw up and form a dome if a circle is hooked too tightly.

Beginners often struggle with twisted strips as they learn how to manipulate them under the surface. After all, you're doing this blind and relying on the feel of the strip. The twisting can happen sometimes because the strips are thin or the texture of the wool is loose and your fingers can't feed it smoothly without having it twist. Usually this twisting goes away as you develop a sensitivity to how the strips feel in your fingers.

Sometimes a strip pulls apart and breaks. If this happens, pull the last end up to the surface, trim it off evenly, discard the broken strip, and start a new strip in the same hole as the broken one and continue hooking.

You'll be amazed how quickly you develop a feel for the wool strips and the process of pulling loops. You'll get into a rhythm of pulling up the loops and working across the surface of your rug and then you'll relax and enjoy the whole art of rug hooking.

Remember, practice really does make perfect. Draw some straight lines, some circles, some curvy and wavy lines and practice hooking them until you feel comfortable with the consistency of your loops and rows. And don't be too strict with yourself as you're learning. Give yourself time, have fun, and create something beautiful!

Rug Hooking Books

There are many good rug hooking books, old and new. Some are still available in libraries or bookstores, some may be available online, and some may be out of print. You never know where an old copy may pop up, so keep your eye out for any of them at garage sales, classic book shops, or even thrift stores. This is only a partial list of what is readily available to you.

- *Basic Rug Hooking*, Alice Beatty
- *Easy Lettering Tips for the Rug Hooker*, Pris Buttler
- *Hooked on the Wild Side*, Elizabeth Black
- *Geometric Hooked Rugs*, Gail Dufresne
- *Shading Flowers: The Complete Guide for Rug Hookers*, Jeanne Field
- *Hook Me a Story*, Deanne Fitzpatrick
- *Hooking Rugs*, Lila Fretz
- *Pictorial Hooked Rugs*, Jane Halliwell Green
- *Maryanne Lincoln's Comprehensive Dyeing Guide*, Maryanne Lincoln
- *Creative Rug Hooking*, Anne D. Mather
- *Color in Hooked Rugs, The Lore and Lure of Hooked Rugs,* and *You...Can Hook Rugs,* Pearl McGown
- *The Complete Rug Hooker*, Joan Moshimer
- *Everyday Folk Art-Hooked Rugs and Quilts to Make*, Polly Minick
- *Practical Hooked Rugs*, Stella Hay Rex
- *The Rug Hooker's Bible,* Gene Shepherd and Jane Olson
- *The Big Book of Hooked Rugs*, Jessie A. Turbayne

Publications:

- *Rug Beat*, an online magazine, 4 times per year, available through *Rug Hooking* magazine.
- *Rug Hooking* magazine, 5 times per year
- *ATHA Newsletter*, available to ATHA members
- *National Guild of Pearl K. McGown Rughookrafters Newsletter*, available to members
- *Wool Street Journal*, for primitive hookers

Major Woolen Suppliers and Mills

- Dorr Mill, New Hampshire
  www.dorrmill.com,
  (480) 926-7112

- Pendleton, Oregon
  www.pendleton-usa.com,
  (877) 996-6599

- Woolrich, Pennsylvania
  www.woolrich.com,
  (800) 966-5372

- Amana, Iowa
  www.amanashops.com
  (800) 373-6328

- Johnson, Vermont
  www.johnsonwoolenmills.com
  (877) 635-WOOL

- St Peter, Minnesota
  www.woolenmill.com
  (507) 934-3734

- Fingerlakes, New York
  www.fingerlakes-yarns.com
  (315) 497-1542

- Blackberry Ridge, Wisconsin
  www.blackberry-ridge.com
  (608) 437-3762

- The Wool Studio
  www.thewoolstudio.com

- Heavens to Betsy
  www.heavens-to-betsy.com

Dye Brands

Several companies manufacture powdered dyes for wool. The acid dyes are created specifically for animal or protein products like wool, silk, or nylon. Here are some of the more popular brands of dye:

- Aljo
  www.aljodye.com
- Cushing Perfection Dye
  www.cushing.com
- Earthues
  www.earthues.com
- Jacquard
  www.jacquardproducts.com

- Lanaset
  www.earthguild.com
- Majic Carpet Dye (Canada)
  www.letshookrugs.com
- Pro Chem
  www.prochemical.com
- Procion
  www.jacquardproducts.com

References & Resources

- Bee Line-Towsend Industries
  www.beeline-townsend.com, 2011

- Cheticamp Hooked Rugs—Coopérative Artisanale
  www.cheticamphookedrugs.com, 2011

- Grenfell Hooked Mats
  www.grenfellhookedmats.com, 2011

- Harry M. Fraser Company
  www.fraserrugs.com, 2011

- Honeydoo Cutters
  www.honeydoocutters.com, 2011.

- McGown, Pearl K.
  Color in Hooked Rugs. Boston: Buck Printing Co., 1954

- Moshimer, Joan
  The Complete Book of Rug Hooking. Boston: New York Graphic Society, 1975

- Morton, J.L. Color Matters
  www.colormatters.com/colortheory.html

- Munsell Color System.
  http://en.wiki/Munsell_color_system

- Northern New Jersey Chapter 35, *"H" as in Hooking.*
  National Guild of Pearl K. McGown Hookrafters, Inc., 1996

- Phillips, Anna M. Laise. *Hooked Rugs and How to Make Them.*
  New York: The MacMillan Co., 1925

- Rex, Stella Hay. *Practical Hooked Rugs.* Chicago: Ziff Davis Publishing Co., 1949

- Ries, Estelle H. *American Rugs.* Cleveland: The World Publishing Co., 1950

- Ryan, Jennifer A. Esq. "Copyright Law Q &A." *Rug Hooking* Magazine. Vol XV, June, July, Aug 2003:
  pp. 58–60

- Shepherd, Gene, and Jane Olson, *The Rug Hooker's Bible.*
  Lemoyne, PA: *Rug Hooking* Magazine, 2005

- The Oxford Company,
  www.amyoxford.com, 2011

- Bolivar Cutters
  www.bolivarcutter.com, 2011